Sir William Crookes:
A Short Biography

Nineteenth-Century British
Chemist and Spiritualist

Doug West, Ph.D.

For my grandson Isaiah

Table of Contents

Preface

Welcome to the book, *Sir William Crookes: A Short Biography*. This book is volume 35 of the 30 Minute Book Series and, as the name of the series implies, if you are an average reader this book will take around 30 minutes to read. Since this short book is not meant to be an all-encompassing biography of William Crookes, you may want to know more about this man and his accomplishments. To help you with this, there are several good references at the end of this book. I have also provided a Timeline, in order to link together the important events in Crookes' life, and a section titled "Biographical Sketches," which includes brief biographies of some of the key individuals in the book.

Thank you for purchasing this book, and I hope you enjoy your time reading about this legendary nineteenth-century scientist.

Doug West
January 2019

Introduction

During his long career, the English chemist, Sir William Crookes, was able to make significant contributions to photography, chemistry, physics, agricultural science, public health, and scientific journalism. He had a talent for investigating the unusual, which probably brought him to the study of psychic phenomenon. Historians of science have recognized Crookes for his brilliance as an experimental researcher and his controversial support for spiritualistic phenomena; however, he made his living primarily as a science journalist and editor. His interests were eclectic, ranging from pure and applied science, economic and practical problems, and psychic research. He is credited with the discovery of the element thallium and invention of the Crookes tube and the radiometer. He held patents on early light bulbs and his improvements in vacuum pump technology were key to the development of electric lighting and the discovery of the X-ray. His wide range of interests and prolific publication of his and others' works made him a well-known personality within the late Victorian era scientific community. He gained worldwide acclaim in his 1898 British Association address, in which he discussed the desperate need to fix nitrogen to solve the perceived future world food shortage. His address was twice published and reported in many of the world's leading newspapers and spurred the development of artificial fertilizer.

Chapter 1 - Early Years

"The spectroscope reveals that the elementary components of the stars and the earth are pretty much the same." – William Crookes

William Crookes was born in London on June 17, 1832. He was the eldest of sixteen children of a successful tailor who had become wealthy through a series of shrewd real estate deals. When Crookes was only five years old, in 1837, the news broke of the possibility that images of nature could be fixed chemically on glass and paper using a lens and chemical compounds. The young boy became fascinated by the new science of photography and began to experiment with this new technology from an early age.

Just around the corner from his father's tailor shop was the Royal College of Chemistry, where he became a full time student at age 16. Within a year, Crookes had won a scholarship to continue his studies, and within two years he had become the personal assistant to the director, August Hofmann. The Royal College of Chemistry produced few academic chemists; the majority of its graduates became industrial chemists or consultants. At the college, he developed a close friendship with another of Hofmann's personal assistants, John Spiller, who was also very interested in photography. To improve their photographic techniques, the two young chemists spent weekends and holidays together experimenting with different cameras, paper, and chemical processes. Their collaboration would continue years after Crookes left the Royal College of Chemistry. Attending a meeting of the Royal Society with Hofmann, Crookes met the eminent scientist Michael Faraday, who encouraged him to pursue the new fields of optical photography and later spectroscopy rather than pure chemistry. Crookes decided to make a career for himself as an independent consultant specializing in photographic science.

After leaving college in 1854, he became an assistant at the Radcliffe Observatory, Oxford. At the observatory he was the sole member of the Meteorological Department. He worked on the development of instruments that would provide an automatic hourly recording of weather conditions. Crookes made improvements in recording techniques, chiefly by using waxed photographic paper. His technique was adopted by the Royal Society's observatory at Kew Gardens and would form the basis of his first book published in 1857 and titled *A Handbook of the Waxed Paper Process in Photography.*

After a short stay of a year at Oxford, Crookes took up a new career as a schoolteacher in Chester. The school was a training college for students who intended to become teachers in the National Schools. Affairs of the heart would interrupt his stay at Chester as he fell in love and the school would not employ married teachers. He met Ellen Humphrey while spending his weekends in Liverpool where he was taking photographs of the moon and other celestial objects using a telescope that had been established on the harbor front. The couple married and moved to London in 1856; they had ten children and remained married until the death of Ellen in 1916. Ellen would be a very important part of Crookes' scientific life, as well as his personal. When needed, she would weigh chemicals, assist with investigations, and was a constant source of encouragement for his endeavors.

Crookes was very interested in photography and made significant contributions, including the development of the dry plate through the use of deliquescent chemicals, the recycling of fused collodion, the development of waxed paper techniques, and the determination of the spectral sensitivities of chemically saturated papers. He brought scientific rigor to the new science of photography and is especially remembered for his pioneering lunar photographs.

Crookes became editor of *The Journal of the Liverpool & Manchester Photographic Society* as well as secretary of the London Photographic Society and editor of their journal. His position at the Photographic Society didn't go well, and he was accused of misappropriation of the society's funds and fired. He quickly found work as editor of the *Photographic News*, a weekly journal dedicated to the burgeoning field of photography. Initially things went well for Crookes in the position, but then trouble started and he was fired in December 1859. He sued the publisher of *Photographic News* for wrongful termination but lost the court case based on the inflammatory remarks he had published against his previous employers at the London Photographic Society, and because he had founded a rival journal, *Chemical News*, without his employer's permission.

With his career as a photographic chemist on the wane, he turned his attention to building the readership of the *Chemical News* and enhancing his reputation as an analytical chemist. *Chemical News* was not his only venture in publishing. From 1863 to 1879, he was the editor of the *Quarterly Science Review*. This journal provided Crookes and other scientific contributors the opportunity to write popular and authoritative accounts of contemporary scientific developments. This publication was also a forum to mold public opinion on civic problems of the day—water purity, sewage disposal, and agricultural productivity.

While the *Chemical News* would remain one of his main sources of income for the remainder of his life, he also supplemented his income through publications of chemical handbooks and work as a consultant. His income also came from advice that he provided on sanitary matters, such as the disposal of town sewage and water purification. *Chemical News* gave him a weekly platform to bolster his career as a consultant. One of his best-known analytical handbooks was the *Select Methods of Chemical Analysis* published in 1871. This became an essential reference book in libraries of public analysts. Crookes was instrumental in the development of societies and journals that promoted the expansion of public education of chemistry. Professional chemical associations like the Society for Public Analysts, the Institute of Chemistry, and the Society for Chemical Industry can trace their origins back through the editorial support that Crookes gave them in *Chemical News*.

Chapter 2 – Scientific Investigations and Discoveries

"The phenomena in these exhausted tubes reveal to physical science a new world—a world where matter may exist in a fourth state, where the corpuscular theory of light may be true, and where light does not always move in straight lines, but where we can never enter, and with which we must be content to observe and experiment from the outside." – William Crookes

In 1859, the pair of German scientists Robert Bunsen and Gustav Kirchhoff announced the invention of the spectroscope, a device that broke down light with the aid of a glass prism into its constituent colors. Each chemical element had its own series of spectral lines; thus, this allowed the identification of known elements in a sample. Brunsen and Kirchhoff used their spectroscope to detect two previously unknown elements, cesium and rubidium. Crookes immersed himself in spectroscopy and became skilled in the field, and it was not long before instrument makers were asking him for design specifications. Crookes began to search for new elements by taking the spectrum of samples from his private collection of minerals. In 1861, his efforts were rewarded when he detected a previously unknown green spectral line in a sample of selenium ore. He named the new element thallium in May 1862. He exhibited minute samples of thallium, in the form of a black powder and its salts, the following month at the International Exhibition that was held in South Kensington.

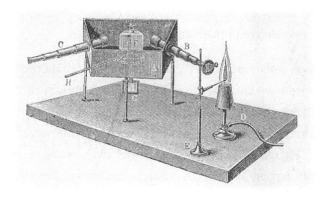

Figure - Spectroscope of Kirchhoff and Bunsen.

Crookes' discovery of thallium soon turned controversial when a French chemist also announced he had isolated thallium. As is often the case in simultaneous discoveries, the glory of the find took on nationalistic overtones. British chemists rushed to protect Crookes' honor by electing him to the Royal Society in 1863. At least in the eyes of the British scientific community, this gave Crookes the purview to take the lead to investigate thallium to determine its exact physical and chemical properties.

Crookes began to investigate the properties of thallium, which would require the utmost accuracy in his measurements. He took great care to purify his reagents, to calibrate his weights, and to use an extremely sensitive Oertling balance, which he mounted in an iron case where most of the air could be removed. This increased the accuracy. In 1873, he published the atomic weight of thallium was 203.642.

It was while operating the vacuum balance that Crookes noticed an unusual effect that the equilibrium of the balance was slightly changed by differences in the temperature between samples. He noted that warmer bodies appeared lighter than colder ones. If the results were not obtained under vacuum conditions, the effect could have been caused by the condensation of vapor on the colder sample, or by air currents surrounding the hotter body. He was confused as to the exact cause of the difference. Crookes felt he had stumbled upon some mysterious link between heat and gravitation.

Crookes found that when a large mass was brought near a smaller mass suspended in an evacuated chamber, it was either attracted or repelled. To examine the effect in detail, he mounted two pith balls on a pivoted horizontal rod in a tube attached to a mercury vacuum pump. He found that the attraction or repulsion was heightened when the pressure was decreased. To investigate this phenomenon, Crookes had to develop pumps and glass apparatus capable of producing a vacuum of approximately one-millionth of an atmosphere. His great strides forward in improving vacuum technology allowed for the development of electric light bulbs and X-ray tubes. Crookes came to the conclusion that the movement of the pith balls in the evacuated chamber was produced by the repulsive force due to radiation from warm bodies. He mistakenly assumed the effect was due to the pressure of light, as predicted by James Maxwell's theory. Using this idea, Crookes constructed a "light-mill" or "radiometer," which was a form of radiation detector in 1875.

The radiometer is a small evacuated glass bulb containing an arrangement of four lightweight metal vanes situated on the head of a pin that are allowed to rotate horizontally. Alternate sides of the vanes are polished or blackened. When light or a form of radiant heat falls on the instrument, the vanes begin to rotate. The rotation of the vanes depends on the low gas pressure in the bulb; molecules leaving the dark or hotter surface have greater momentum than those leaving the bright or cooler surfaces. When the radiometer was placed near a source of light the arms rotated with a speed roughly proportional to the inverse square of the distance between the radiometer and the light. The direction of the vane rotation usually occurred in a direction opposite of that expected if light pressure was the cause. The mechanism causing the vane rotation would be the source of considerable scientific investigation.

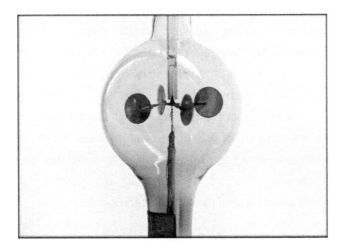

Figure – Crookes' Radiometer.

The mystery behind the inner workings of the radiometer soon caught the attention of some of the top theoretical physicists in Britain, who concluded the motion was caused by the internal movements of molecules in the residual gas in the radiometer vessel. If the mean free path—the distance a gas molecule travels before it collides with another molecule—of the gas is small compared to the dimension of the vessel, molecules that strike the warmer black vanes will rebound with higher velocity and as a result collide with and hold back any slower-moving molecules that are advancing towards the vanes. As a result, a relatively large number of molecules will hit the cooler, unblackened surfaces and prevent any rotation of the vanes. When the pressure is lowered sufficiently, there will come a point at which the mean free path of the molecules will be large enough to prevent compensation of the recoil effect; hence, rotation will occur with the blackened surfaces receding.

Since Crookes was not a mathematical physicist; he left the theoretical explanation of the motion of the vanes up to men like James Maxwell and others. Crookes did continue to investigate the radiometer as he plotted the trajectories of the particles in the vessel by incorporating electrons into the radiometer and tracing the end points of their collisions by using a zinc sulfide screen. Crookes' exacting set of measurements made between 1877 and 1881 showed how the movement of the radiometer confirmed Maxwell's prediction that the viscosity of a gas was independent of its pressure except at the highest exhaustions.

***

In 1878 Crookes began a new area of research related to his work on the radiometer. He was of the conviction "that this dark space coating [the cathode in low-pressure electrical discharges] was in some way related to the layer of molecular pressure causing movement of the radiometer." His investigations of electrical discharges in gases at low pressure produced an improved vacuum tube, known as a Crookes Tube. The Crookes Tube consisted of a glass tube with two electrodes inserted and nearly all the air removed from the tube. When a high voltage is applied across the electrodes the tube begins to glow as the cathode rays fill the tube. Crookes systematically investigated the cathode rays and found that they traveled in straight lines, and when a small object was placed in the path of the radiation it cast a sharp shadow in the fluorescence at the end of the tube. Crookes placed a strong magnet near the tube and found the cathode rays were bent by the magnet, and he concluded that they were particles rather than electromagnetic radiation. Two decades later, the British physicist, JJ Thomson would determine that the cathode rays were electrons.

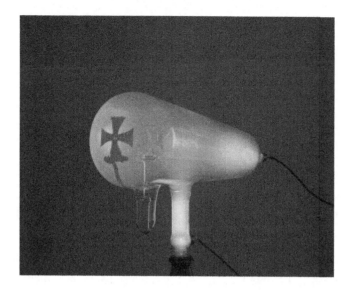

Figure – Crookes Tube showing the shadow of a Maltese Cross cast by the cathode rays.

From his work on cathode rays inside the Crookes Tube, in 1879 he declared, "In studying this fourth-state of matter we seem at length to have within our grasp and obedient to our control the little indivisible particles which with good warrant are supposed to constitute the physical basis of the Universe." Until JJ Thomson verified that cathode rays were indeed electrons, Crookes' theory of a fourth-state of matter was severely criticized by the German school of physicists, who had an alternate view of the nature of cathode rays.

Chapter 3 - Spiritualism

"We are on the track and are not daunted, and fain would we enter the mysterious region which ignorance tickets 'Unknown.'" – William Crookes

In the late 1840s in America, a new movement started called "spiritualism." A spiritualist sought to make contact with the dead through a medium, who was a person believed to have the ability to communicate with the spirits of the dead. In a séance, those hoping to communicate with their dearly departed loved one gathered around the medium while the medium went into a trance-like state, and the spirit world announced their presence through some sort of physical manifestation, such as a sound or movement. Mediums were typically female as they were deemed to be more honest and better at communicating with the spirit world. By the 1860s spiritualism had become common in Europe as it appealed to all classes of people.

William Crookes was initially a sceptic of the spiritualism movement when it came to England; his attitude would take an abrupt about-face upon the death of his younger brother, Philip, at sea in 1867. The younger Crookes had dreams of following his older brother into a technical profession and had been working on a ship laying a telegraph cable from Florida to Cuba. On a visit to Havana with a group of his fellow workers, Phillip contracted yellow fever and died on the voyage back to England. Philips's letters home during his voyage told a story of harsh treatment and exceedingly hard work to the point of exhaustion. William was outraged about the death of his brother and made public accusations against the company that ran the expedition. The accusations landed Crookes in court as the company sued him for libel. After much legal wrangling, Crookes got off with only a small fine.

In the depths of depression over the death of his brother, Crookes sought solace in the spirit world. The year after his brother's death, he told a close scientific friend of "some very extraordinary occurrences" he had witnessed, of spirits of the departed, and these could not be explained by any known physical force. The death of Philip not only troubled William but the larger Crookes family also, and they sought comfort by attending séances to contact Phillip. The experience of the death of his brother appeared to have pushed Crookes to take up the study of mediums and their supposed powers in a scientific manner. Crookes' state of anxiety was exacerbated by his frustration with the erratic behavior of his vacuum balance in his search for the atomic number of thallium. Just as the arms of his super sensitive balance seemed to move by some unknown force, maybe the spirit world held the key for him to come to grips with his brother's death and the strange measurements he was encountering in his laboratory. It was during this time that he would meet the attractive young medium Florence Cook—she would nearly be his undoing.

Now on a mission to understand this new mystical realm, Crookes threw himself into study of the occult, mediums, and psychic powers. He and his wife, Ellen, traveled to Paris and attended several séances ran by notable mediums. The Crookes made friends with the telegraphy engineer Cromwell Varley and his clairvoyant wife, Ada. Varley had taken a keen interest in spiritualism since the early 1850s and suggested there was a strong link between reported spirit induced mechanical movements and electrical force. Varley was a believer in spiritualism and was convinced that he could use his electrical experience to uncover the link between the physical and spiritual realms. Crookes professed an open mind to the validity or absurdity of communication with the dead but in reality, his correspondence of that period reveals a man obsessed with proving the occult was real. After his death, almost all of his "spiritualist" letters were carefully destroyed by his family; however, the few that escaped destruction imply his reading of the occult literature, and his human connections in that realm show he was a man with a belief in the co-existence with *Homo sapiens* of other beings, or demons.

The Investigation of the Medium Daniel Home

Crookes' first serious scientific investigation of spiritualism was with the known medium Daniel Home. Home was born in Scotland in 1833 and moved with his aunt to Connecticut as a young boy. There he became a medium and spiritualist. Finding American audiences growing bored with his show of spiritual powers, he moved to London in 1855. Home proved to be a master showman and a publicity hound. Up until 1862 Home roamed the courts of Europe and Russia casting his mystical spell on those who would have him. Home initiated a meeting with Crookes when he learned of the scientist's interests in spirituality. The two met in 1869 and both Crookes and his wife were charmed with Home's good manners and apparent honesty.

Between 1870 and 1873, Crookes hosted numerous séances with Home. Most of the sessions were in the presence of many members of Crookes' immediate family, some other mediums, and a few other invited guests. Most of the reports from the sessions were of levitations, raps, and the movement of tables, chairs, and small objects. At three of the séances the face or spirit of Philip Crookes was reported. Over a decade later Crookes would write up the events of a dozen of these séances and report them to the Society for Psychical Research.

Mr. Home gave permission for Crookes to investigate his psychic powers in a laboratory. In this case, the laboratory was Crookes' first floor dining room. The windows had been fitted with heavy shutters to keep light and noise out for daytime séances. Since Crookes was in the middle of his dilemma over the anonymous readings he was getting on his research into the atomic weight of thallium, he devised an experiment with Mr. Home that involved a spring scale. In the experiment, a thick wood plank was attached to a spring balance that was suspended from a laboratory tripod while the other end of the plank rested on the dining table. Mr. Home's fingers were placed on the end of the plank before the fulcrum and, on exerting his psychic powers, a depression of the spring balance from two pounds to as much as eight pounds was recorded by the observers. Testing the result himself, Crookes put his full weight on the spot where Home's finger had been, and he was only able to depress the balance to around four pounds. Crookes attributed this increase in weight not to any false movements from Home, but rather to a genuine flow of nervous energy or "psychic force" from Home's body. To confirm what had happened in Crookes' mind, Mr. Home was clearly exhausted, indicating that the law of conservation of energy had been obeyed.

Figure – Daniel Dunglas Home.

After the apparent success of his experiments, there was another one involving the playing of an accordion enclosed in a wire cage. Crookes was anxious to report to the scientific community his discovery of the new "psychic force." Crookes wrote up his findings and submitted a paper to the Royal Society in June of 1871. The secretaries of the Royal Society were clearly embarrassed by Crookes' work and unwilling to publish any "experimental" results that were obtained during a séance. News of Crookes' experiments quickly became public. A month after Crookes' submission to the Royal Society, *The Spectator* reported that Crookes' latest paper had been rejected on the grounds of its "entire want of scientific precision in the evidence adduced." After a second paper was submitted to the British Association, and rejected, Crookes published his experiments with Mr. Home in his *Quarterly Journal* in October 1871.

Crookes' experiments with Mr. Home stirred up a whirlwind of controversy. He now had many detractors and few supporters in the larger scientific community. A few of Crookes' associates who were "believers," such as Varley, came to his aid by writing articles in support of his experimentation. Crookes realized the Home affair had hurt his reputation with his fellow scientists and quickly set back to work on the strictly scientific pursuit of determination of the atomic weight of thallium. This debacle did not diminish Crookes' interest in psychic phenomena; however, he was much more careful in the future to publish work only in the spiritualist, rather than in scientific, publications. That fall, Mr. Home married his second wife, a rich Russian woman he had met in St. Petersburg, and the couple moved to Paris. Much has been written over the years to explain the ways in which Mr. Home had deceived the séance sitters and William Crookes.

The Spirit of Florence Cook

Through dedicated effort, Crookes and his assistant were able to redeem themselves in the eyes of the Royal Society with the measurement of thallium's atomic mass and the invention of the radiometer. With Daniel Home out of the picture, Crookes looked for another medium to work with and study. He and his wife began attending séances in the modest home of the Cook family on the east end of London. The medium was Cook's pretty dark-haired daughter Florence, who had just turned sixteen in the summer of 1872. Florence had been working at a school as a tutor but was dismissed when her work as a spiritualist became public. Like many young Victorian women with few prospects, being a medium provided a career and income. By the spring of 1872, Florence had conjured up the phantom she called "Katie King." At this point Florence was becoming a known medium in the spiritualist circles of London. Her benefactor and promoter, Charles Blackburn, contacted Crookes and asked if he could validate Miss Cook's credentials as a medium. Crookes willingly took on the project to investigate the manifestation of Katie King by Florence. Florence visited the Crookes' home on Mornington Road in northwest London frequently to give Crookes

23

the opportunity to study the young medium and work with her. The Crookes household was a bustling place, with their nine children, a tenth on the way, Crookes' mother-in-law living with them, and domestic help coming and going.

In 1874, Crookes began to test Florence and was able to take several photographs of the manifestation of Katie King. During one séance, Cook was behind a curtain lying on a sofa with a shawl wrapped about her face. Then Katie appeared in front of the curtain where Crookes checked to be sure that Cook was still lying on the sofa. Crookes reported that Cook was still on the sofa; however, he didn't acknowledge that he lifted the shawl to verify it was Cook still on the sofa. With Crookes' expertise in photography, he was able to capture over fifty images of the spiritual apparition Katie. Only a few of the photos have survived as many were destroyed shortly before his death in 1919.

Figure – William Crookes with Katie King.

As with the investigation of Mr. Home, Crookes immediately fell under criticism from the non-believers. Skeptics contended the similarities in the appearance of Katie and Florence were simply because they were the same person. Theories abound as to why Crookes was so lax with his scientific method in his research in the Cook-King collaboration. Some say he was seduced by the charms of the young woman and let his guard down, and apparently there was another young woman working with Florence. Others argued that he was such a strong believer in the spirit world, and he was very nearsighted, that he simply reported what he wanted to see. And there is always the explanation the whole thing was real, that Katie King was some supernatural apparition conjured from the mist by Miss Cook!

After about two years of working with Crookes, Florence informed him that she had been recently married and was giving up on being a medium. Florence would stay in retirement for six years and then only make occasional appearances at séances as a lively singing and dancing spirit named Marie.

Crookes was overwhelmed with criticism from the scientific community, so much so that he temporarily stopped his active research into psychic forces. He did remain an active investigator of spiritualism until his death. He claimed to be widely read in "Spiritualism, Demonology, Witchcraft, Animal Magnetism, Spiritual Theology, Magic and Medical Psychology in English, French, and Latin." Upon its founding in 1882, he joined the Society for Psychical Research and became the president of the organization in 1897. Crookes was always skeptical of the spirit world and sometimes gullible, but he never believed the spiritualistic séances presented unequivocal evidence that "spirits" were those of human dead. He is perhaps best described as an occultist, a man for whom traditional science left high areas of creation unexposed. His belief in spiritualism did not seem to have affected his positive view of Christianity, as he and Ellen were regular churchgoers throughout their lives.

Chapter 4 - Electric Lighting

"Which was first, Matter or Force? If we think on this question, we shall find that we are unable to conceive of matter without force, or force without matter. When God created the elements of which the earth is composed, He created certain wondrous forces, which are set free and become evident when matter acts on matter." – William Crookes

Crookes and his assistant Charles Gimingham became aware of the fact that their knowledge of vacuum technology would be useful in the manufacture of an electric incandescent lamp. This would be an improvement over the electric arc lamp because its filament would wear out more slowly. Both electric lighting systems had the advantage over gas illumination, which consumed the oxygen in a room and caused headaches. Electric lighting would be handier, in that it could be turned on and off with the flick of a switch. The question came down to economics: Could the incandescent light bulb and the necessary electrical infrastructure compete with the well-established gas illumination? Crookes was not the only one in pursuit of the possibility of developing a practical electric light. His two most notable competitors were Thomas Edison in

America and Joseph Swan in England. The electric lighting of 1879 came in two basic types, an arc-lighting lamp system and the incandescent glow lamps that Crookes and Swan were experimenting with.

Crookes' breakthrough for the incandescent lamp came when, with the assistance of Gimingham, he investigated the glow behavior of a platinum coil inserted inside a radiometer bulb while connected to a battery. The bulb worked and produced a steady light whose intensity depended on the amount of voltage applied to the bulb. The problem was that the platinum filament was very expensive and burnt out in a few hours, making it a working electric light but not practical for the domestic market. Crookes, Swan, and Edison were all faced with the same dilemma: What material to use for the bulb filament that was inexpensive and would burn for hours? The hunt was on. By this point Edison was an on his way to becoming a very successful inventor and industrialist, far exceeding the reach and capabilities of Swan or Crookes. Gimingham and Crookes continued to perfect the lamp and in 1881 Crookes received four patents on electric lighting. It was about this time that Crookes lost his trusted and very capable assistant Gimingham to Swan. Gimingham had just married and needed a larger salary than Crookes could provide. The two frontrunners in the race to a practical electric lamp were clearly Swan and Edison; rather than compete, they joined forces and formed the

Edison & Swan United Electric Light Company.

Crookes began to make lights bulbs in his own factory in Battersea. There, Crookes and his son Henry, along with a new assistant James Gardiner, pursued research on the design of a long-lasting bulb filament. Crookes made a fruitless contact with an American company wanting to break into the American market for electric lamps. Crookes was not in the league of entrepreneur like Swan and Edison, and he sought to sell his patents to the pair. In 1889, Crookes abandoned the Battersea lamp factory, sold the assets, and sent Henry to South Africa to see whether he could make his fortune in the gold fields using his father's improved methods of extraction of gold.

Crookes used the bulbs and equipment to electrify his new house in Kensington Park Gardens. A gas-powered generator was housed in the basement to provide the electrical power for the light bulbs. With this arrangement, he was able to power twenty electric lamps at the same time in his home, making his home the first electric house in London.

Although Crookes only played a small part in the development of the electric lighting, he was an essential character in the story. Without the glass-blowing and vacuum systems that he and his assistant Charles Gimingham developed while pursuing their radiometric research, the development of the electric light bulb would have been delayed for years, if not decades. Crookes remained involved with electricity and started a company to light the Notting Hill district of London where he lived, and he remained the director of the company for the remainder of his life.

With Crookes at the forefront of the development of electricity, it was natural that he would become the President of the Institute of Electrical Engineers in 1891. In this role, Crookes was involved in hosting diners, and at one of these, at the Piccadilly Hotel in November 1891, he delivered an important speech that contained some startling predictions for the future of electric power. He speculated that we had only discovered a small portion of the electromagnetic spectrum and that in the future we would be able to transmit intelligence over these waves; hence, he envisioned radio and television in the modern world. Crookes continued, "Rays of light will not pass through a wall, nor, as we know only too well, through dense fog. But electrical rays of a foot or two wave-length...will easily pierce such mediums, which for them will be transparent." He urged electrical engineers to develop better ways of generating electric waves of precise wavelength, of sending them out in a specific direction, and of receiving them at precisely defined wavelengths. Crookes was met with some criticism for his far-reaching ideas on the future of electricity; however, his critics were proved wrong when in 1893, the extraordinary Croatian engineer Nikola Tesla gave a lecture on how such a wireless apparatus might be constructed. Within a year after Tesla's lecture, the wireless transmission of signal was demonstrated. Based on Crookes' foresight, he has been awarded the distinction by history of predicting the advent of radio communication. In a rather odd bit of historical trivia, Guglielmo Marconi, the inventor of the radio, had settled in the Notting Hill area and was Crookes's neighbor.

Chapter 5 – Research Continues

"It is the chemist who must come to the rescue of the threatened communities. It is through the laboratory that starvation may ultimately be turned to plenty."
– William Crookes

Agricultural matters were always an interest to Crookes. This probably stemmed from his days at the Royal College of Chemistry, which had been endowed by agricultural interests. On becoming president of the British Association for the Advancement of science in 1898, he used that position to express his views on science and the occult, and to warn the world of an impending food shortage coming in the next few decades due to the failure of wheat production to keep up with the growing world population. Crookes placed the responsibility of developing new fertilizers on chemists, particularly the problem of tapping the enormous supply of atmospheric nitrogen that could be used for fertilizer. His remarks were viewed as sensationalism by many; however, they did cause a stir among scientists, economists, and politicians. Crookes' campaign was a factor in the motivation that drove O.C. Birkeland and Fritz Haber to develop industrial processes for nitrogen fixation, resulting in a source of inexpensive fertilizer.

After the discovery of radioactivity by Henry Becquerel in 1895, Crookes began to investigate the strange properties of the radioactive element uranium. At age sixty-eight, he was not ready for retirement and threw himself into the study of newly uncovered perplexing problems associated with radioactivity. The property of radioactive decay, where one substance spontaneously changes into another over time, confounded Crookes, and everyone else, as he felt the underlying process must violate the principle of conservation of energy. In 1900 he found that a solution of uranium salt could be treated chemically so as to precipitate a small quantity of the more highly radioactive substance in the salt. The uranium left in the solution only had a low level of radiation when compared to the more radioactive precipitate. Crookes initially thought that the radioactivity of uranium was not from the uranium but rather from an impurity.

In 1903, Crookes showed that a particular type of radiation given off by radioactive material, known as alpha particles, would cause a screen coated with zinc sulfide to luminesce and that when using a microscope this luminescence consisted of a multitude of individual flashes. Crookes had invented the spinthariscope, Greek for "spark viewer." This device would be very important a few years later when Ernest Rutherford made groundbreaking discoveries on the makeup of the atom using Crookes' device. In 1900, Crookes confided to a friend that be believed radioactivity was due to "bodies smaller than atoms." And by 1906, he had fully accepted Ernest Rutherford's subatomic transmutation theory of radioactivity.

Chapter 6 – The Sage of Chemical Physics

"The task I am called upon to perform today is to my thinking by no means a merely formal or easy matter. It fills me with deep concern to give an address, with such authority as a president's chair confers, upon a science which, though still in a purely nascent stage, seems to me at least as important as any other science whatever. Psychical science, as we here try to pursue it, is the embryo of something which in time may dominate the whole world of thought." – William Crookes

Crookes had now reached the status of the elder statesman of British science and was awarded the Order of Merit in 1910 and chosen as president of the Royal Society in 1913. Since Lord Kelvin's death in 1907, Crookes had become Britain's most visible and respected living scientist. For his crowning achievement in science he was elected president of the most prestigious scientific organization, the Royal Society. His first major event was to host the large annual dinner at the Hotel Metropole in December 1913. As was the custom, the president gave a speech highlighting some aspect of science and society. Crookes chose to speak about the relationship between science and the government. He opined that the Royal Society needed more money from the government and philanthropists for the organization's many deserving projects. At the June meeting of the next year, one of the members wrote of Crookes and his wife, "The President stood remarkably erect for his eighty-two years, and wore the Order of Merit on its blue ribbon. He was, as a matter of fact, five feet, 8-1/2 inches in height, having lost about an inch in the preceding ten years. Lady Crookes [who had been unwell for days] had no airs of the *grande dame*, but her greeting seemed to convey a genuine welcome. They seemed both to be enjoying the novel dignity of the occasion."

Well past his eightieth birthday, Crookes' career in science and industry was not over; he was busy on an important piece of applied research on glass. He was working on a type of glass for spectacles worn to protect the eyes of workers exposed to dangerous industrial processes. Workers in such industries as glass-making and iron smelting were experiencing eye damage from the glare of the hot furnaces. Crookes had extensive experience with glass blowing and spectroscopy and was searching for the formula for a type of glass that could be used to protect the eyes of the workers. He experimented with different types of glass at his home laboratory and at the Whitefriars glass works. On-site spectroscopic analysis of the light emitted from the furnaces revealed that furnace workers received a massive dose of infrared radiation into their eyes each day at work.

During the summer of 1911, Crookes reported his results of investigating about 160 different combinations of glass. After two more years of research, at the end of 1913 he published a formulation that cut off ninety percent of the heat radiation, was opaque to ultraviolet light, and was nearly free of color distortion. He noted that there would be an additional advantage if tinting were added to the glass, allowing it to be used to reduce glare to those exposed to bright light conditions, such as reflected sunlight off snow or the ocean or bright electric lights. Crookes was not the first to develop a tinted lens for leisure use, but his innovation was the forerunner of modern sunglasses. Once the news of the new type of glass became public, Crookes and Gardiner were inundated with inquiries from the public and glass manufacturers wanting to make the new formulation. World War I interrupted the push for the production of the new glass, but by 1920, large scale production of the protective glasses was in place and they were frequently called "Crookes Lenses."

Figure – Sir William Crookes.

The outbreak of World War I, in August of 1914, caught Crookes and his wife by surprise as they had just begun their annual vacation with their banker and business partner. With their vacation cut short, they returned to London. A call came out from the government to the Royal Society to provide guidance on how to boost industrial production and develop ingenious new weapons to support the war effort. Under Crookes' guidance, the Royal Society set up a War Committee to assist the military and industry to combat the Germans. The additional pressure of the war on Crookes' workload left him weary. The ceaseless rounds of committee meetings, dinners, and speeches took its toll on even his strong constitution. With the additional burden of his wife's failing health, he realized he could no longer keep up this pace. Sensibly, he handed over the reins of the Royal Society to the younger and very capable JJ Thomson, who was 59 years old.

Free of the heavy responsibilities of the Royal Society, Crookes returned to his spectroscopy. He began to study the composition of meteorites from the collection of the British Museum. A personal tragedy struck the family when their older son, Henry, died of malaria in 1915. William and Ellen took the death of Henry very hard. Ellen's health continued to decline and on May 10, 1916, she died in her eighty-first year. She was buried in the family grave with the epitaph, "Earth holds one gentle woman less and heaven one angel more." Crookes was devastated with the death of his wife. She had been his nearly constant companion for six decades and had weathered the many storms of life with him. Crookes retreated into his inner sanctum, his laboratory, and continued his investigations into spectroscopy.

Friends of Crookes started to notice a decline in his health, noting he had become very frail and suggested food no longer appealed to him, though he continued to smoke cigarettes. Pursuing his work until the very end, he died in his sleep in his Notting Hill house on April 4, 1919. James Gardiner announced his death to the readers of the *Chemical News*, accompanied by the last photograph of him ever taken. According to Gardiner, Crookes never recovered from his wife's death: "Gradually his strength gave way, and the writer, watching him, saw a daily added feebleness; but there was never a murmur or word of complaint, always the same kindly greeting and pleasant smile, until physical weakness gained the upper hand and he passed quietly away in the early hours of the morning." His funeral was conducted at St. John's Church, the church that he and his family had attended since the 1880s. The service was attended by family, friends, representatives from all of London's learned societies, business associates, and the mayor of Kensington.

So ended the life of a remarkable man who had accomplished so much without the benefit of a university education or academic position. He attained a position of scientific leadership through his hard work and dedication to his craft, which culminated in the presidency of the Royal Society. He earned a living and supported his large family working as a chemical analyst, consultant, and editor, with nearly all of his research conducted in his home laboratory. Today we can remember Sir William Crookes for his advancement of our knowledge of the subatomic world, the television tube and computer monitor, until they were replaced by liquid crystal display system, and the ubiquitous pair of sunglasses.

The End

Thank you for purchasing the book. I hope you enjoyed reading it. Please don't forget to leave a review of the book. I read each one and they help me become a better writer.

- Doug

Timeline

June 17, 1832 – Born in London, England. Eldest of sixteen children.

1848 – Enters the Royal College of Chemistry in London.

1850 to 1854 – Assistant to A.W. Hofmann at the Royal College of Chemistry.

1854 – Assistant at the Radcliffe Observatory in Oxford.

1856 – Marries Ellen Humphrey. Teaches chemistry at College of Science at Chester.

1857 – Publishes first book, *A Handbook to the Waxed Paper Process in Photography*.

September 1858 – Editor of the *Photographic News*.

1859 – Starts journal *Chemical News*.

1861 – Discovers thallium spectroscopically.

1862 – Names new element thallium.

1863 – Elected to the Royal Society.

1871 – Published book *Select Methods of Chemical Analysis.*

1875 – Invents the radiometer.

1882 – Joined the Society for Psychical Research.

1883 – Becomes member of the Theosophical Society.

1891 – Elected president of the Institute of Electrical Engineers.

1897 – President of Society for Psychical Research. Knighted.

1898 – Elected president of the British Association for the Advancement of Science.

1909 – Publishes book on diamonds.

1910 – Receives Order of Merit.

1916 – Ellen Crookes dies.

April 4, 1919 – Dies in London.

Biographical Sketches

<u>Becquerel, Henri</u> (1852-1908) French physicist. Becquerel was born in Paris. His early scientific and engineering training was at the Ecole Polytechnique and the School of Bridges and Highways. After completing his doctorate, he became a professor of physics, continuing the family tradition of his father and grandfather. He is most remembered as the discoverer of radioactivity in 1896. Following the discovery of X-rays in 1895, he began researching fluorescence in uranium salts. Through a bit of luck, Becquerel uncovered a new form of radiation coming from the salts, which was later found to be emanating from the nuclear disintegrations in the uranium atoms. In 1903 he shared the Nobel Prize for physics for his work on radioactivity with Pierre and Marie Curie.

<u>Bunsen, Robert</u> (1811-1899) German chemist. Bunsen obtained his doctorate at the university in Gottingen. After teaching at different universities in Germany, he spent the bulk of his teaching and research career at the university in Heidelberg (1852-1889). Bunsen was a great experimentalist with expertise in gas analysis and glass blowing. Along with Gustav Kirchhoff, the pair were pioneers in the science of spectroscopy and discovered the elements rubidium and cesium. In 1855,

Bunsen improved upon the laboratory burner used by Michael Faraday and it became a fixture in chemical laboratories and still bears the name *Bunsen Burner*.

Cook, Florence (1856-1904) British. Claimed to be a medium that could communicate with the dead and materialized the spirit "Katie King." Over the years she was exposed as a fraud.

Edison, Thomas (1847-1931) American physicist and inventor. Born in Milan, Ohio, Edison was home-schooled by his mother. He learned telegraphy as a young man and taught himself about electricity. He set up a laboratory for invention and is credited with invention of the phonograph, the electric light, as well as over 1000 other inventions. He was instrumental in setting up the large scale electrical generation and distribution system for parts of the United States.

Faraday, Michael (1791-1867) British physicist and chemist. Faraday was the son of a blacksmith and grew up poor in England. He received little formal education. The chemist Humphry Davy was key to Faraday's development into a prominent scientist. He spent his career at the Royal Institute in London researching problems in chemistry and electricity. Faraday is most remembered for his work on electrolysis and discovery of the law of electromagnetic induction. Faraday's concept of electrical lines of force would be later fully developed by James Clerk Maxwell and become part of

Maxwell's powerful and rigorous electromagnetic equations.

<u>Hofmann, August</u> (1818-1892) German organic chemist. Educated in chemistry he became the head of London's Royal College of Chemistry in 1845. He became a professor of chemistry in Berlin in 1865. Hofmann was an experimental chemist who, along with his students, developed new organic compounds. He produced hundreds of research papers during his long career. He was married four times and had eleven children.

<u>Home, Daniel</u> (1833-1886) A Scottish medium who reportedly had the ability to levitate, speak to the dead, and produce rapping or knocking sounds in a house at will. Home conducted hundreds of séances attended my many in the United States and Europe.

<u>Kirchhoff, Gustav</u> (1825-1887) German physicist. He was born in Russia and received his formal education at the university in Königsberg. While a student, he formulated Kirchhoff's laws, which refer to the currents and electromotive forces in electrical networks. Along with Robert Bunsen, he discovered the elements cesium and rubidium.

<u>Maxwell, James Clerk</u> (1831-1879) British physicist. Maxwell was born in Edinburgh, Scotland, and studied there and at Cambridge University. Maxwell is regarded as the greatest theoretical physicist of the 19th century.

His work on thermodynamics as well as electricity and magnetism formed a mathematical formulation of the two disciplines. Maxwell was the first head of the Cavendish Laboratory at Cambridge University.

Roentgen (or Röntgen), Wilhelm (1845-1923) German physicist. Roentgen was born in Germany and studied at the Zurich Polytechnic. He studied and taught at several German universities. While a physics professor in Würzburg he made his famous discovery of X-rays in 1895. During his work with a Crookes electric discharge tube, he noticed that a screen coated with barium platinocyanide was fluorescing during the experiment. He realized that the cathode rays could not travel more than a few inches and the glowing screen was several feet away, thus he realized he had discovered a new phenomenon. Roentgen's discovery immediately created great interest in the scientific and medical community. Roentgen was awarded the first Nobel prize in physics in 1901.

Rutherford, Ernest (1871-1937) Rutherford was born in New Zealand and won a scholarship to study at Cambridge University in England. He spent most of his career as a university professor in Canada and England studying radioactivity and the nature of the atom. He developed the Rutherford model of the atom. With his associate Hans Geiger, they invented the Geiger counter in 1908 to detect radioactive particles. He was the head of the Cavendish Laboratory at Cambridge University from 1919 until his death. He received the Nobel Prize in chemistry in 1908 for his work on radioactivity.

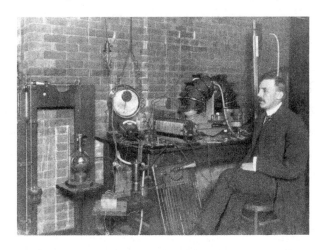

Figure – Ernest Rutherford in his laboratory at McGill University in 1905.

Soddy, Frederick (1877-1956) British chemist. Soddy was born in Eastborne, United Kingdom, and was educated at the University College of Aberystwyth and Oxford Universities. After working with Ernest Rutherford in Canada and William Ramsey in London, he taught chemistry at various universities. Working with Rutherford from 1901 to 1903, they discovered that radioactive elements would change into other elements through a series of stages. He came up with the concept of the isotope, which are chemically identical elements with slightly different atomic numbers. He won the Nobel Prize in 1921 in chemistry for his work on the origins and nature of isotopes. After 1919, he became disillusioned with science and became a writer on social and economic issues.

Swan, Joseph (1828-1914) British chemist, physicist, and inventor. Independent early developer of the incandescent light bulb. Responsible for supplying lighting to many homes in London. Formed a company for electric lighting that merged with that of Thomas Edison to form the Edison & Swan United Electric Light Company, otherwise known as "Ediswan."

Thomson, Joseph John "JJ" (1856-1940) British physicist. Thomson was born in Manchester, United Kingdom, and entered Owens College at age 14 to study engineering and the sciences. He then went to Cambridge University where he graduated in 1876 and remained at the university in various positions until his death. Thomson built the Cavendish Laboratory into a premier research institution. He is most remembered for his work with cathode rays and his determination that they are negatively charged fundamental particles we now call electrons. He received the Nobel Prize in 1906 for his work on the conduction of electricity through gases. He was knighted in 1908.

Varley, Cromwell (1828-1883) British engineer and spiritualist. Varley became the chief engineer of the Electric Telegraphy Company and was involved with the laying of the first transatlantic telegraph cable. Varley was involved in the spiritualist movement and carried out investigations with fellow physicist William Crookes. He was a founding member of the Society of Telegraph Engineers, which became the Institute of Electrical Engineers.

References and Further Reading

Brock, William H. *William Crookes (1832-1919) and the Commercialization of Science*. Ashgate Publishing Limited. 2008.

Gillispie, Charles C. (editor in chief) *Dictionary of Scientific Biography*. Charles Scribner's Sons. 1976.

Daintith, John and Derek Gjertsen (editors). *Oxford Dictionary of Scientists*. Oxford University Press. 1999.

Hall, Trevor H. *The Medium and the Scientist: The Story of Florence Cook and William Crookes*. Prometheus Books. 1984.

Kutler, Stanley I. (editor in Chief) *Dictionary of American History*. Third Edition. Charles Scribner's Sons. 2003.

Millar, David, Ian Millar, John Millar, and Margaret Millar. *The Cambridge Dictionary of Scientists*. Cambridge University Press. 1996.

Patterson, Gary D. and Seth C. Rasmussen (editors). *Charters in Chemistry: A Celebration of the Humanity of Chemistry*. American Chemical Society. 2013.

Acknowledgments

I would like to thank Lisa Zahn for her help in preparation of this book. All pictures are from the public domain. The quotes at the beginning of the chapters are from libquotes.com.

About the Author

Doug West is a retired engineer, small business owner, and experienced writer with several books to his credit. His writing interests are general, with expertise in science, history, biographies, and "How To" topics. Doug has a B.S. in Physics from the Missouri School of Science and Technology and a Ph.D. in General Engineering from Oklahoma State University. He lives with his wife and little dog "Millie" near Kansas City, Missouri. Follow the author on Facebook at: https://www.facebook.com/30minutebooks.

Figure – Doug West (photo by Karina West)

Additional Books by Doug West

Buying and Selling Silver Bullion Like a Pro

How to Write, Publish, and Market Your Own Audio Book

A Short Biography of the Scientist Sir Isaac Newton

A Short Biography of the Astronomer Edwin Hubble

Galileo Galilei – A Short Biography

Benjamin Franklin – A Short Biography

The Astronomer Cecilia Payne-Gaposchkin – A Short Biography

The American Revolutionary War – A Short History

Coinage of the United States – A Short History

John Adams – A Short Biography

In the Footsteps of Columbus (Annotated) Introduction and Biography Included (with Annie J. Cannon)

Alexander Hamilton – Illustrated and Annotated (with Charles A. Conant)

Harlow Shapley – Biography of an Astronomer

Alexander Hamilton – A Short Biography

The Great Depression – A Short History

Jesse Owens, Adolf Hitler and the 1936 Summer Olympics

Thomas Jefferson – A Short Biography

Gold of My Father – A Short Tale of Adventure

Making Your Money Grow with Dividend Paying Stocks – Revised Edition

The French and Indian War – A Short History

The Mathematician John Forbes Nash Jr. – A Short Biography

The British Prime Minister Margaret Thatcher – A Short Biography

Vice President Mike Pence – A Short Biography

President Jimmy Carter – A Short Biography

President Ronald Reagan – A Short Biography

President George H. W. Bush – A Short Biography

Dr. Robert H. Goddard – A Brief Biography - Father of American Rocketry and the Space Age

Richard Nixon: A Short Biography - 37th President of the United States

Charles Lindbergh: A Short Biography - Famed Aviator and Environmentalist

Dr. Wernher von Braun: A Short Biography - Pioneer of Rocketry and Space Exploration

Bill Clinton: A Short Biography – 42nd President of the United States

Joe Biden: A Short Biography - 47th Vice President of the United States

Donald Trump: A Short Biography - 45th President of the United States

Nicolaus Copernicus: A Short Biography - The Astronomer Who Moved the Earth

America's Second War of Independence: A Short History of the War of 1812

John Quincy Adams: A Short Biography - Sixth President of the United States

Andrew Jackson: A Short Biography: Seventh President of the United States

Albert Einstein: A Short Biography Father of the Theory of Relativity

Franklin Delano Roosevelt: A Short Biography: Thirty-Second President of the United States

James Clerk Maxwell: A Short Biography: Giant of Nineteenth-Century Physics

Ernest Rutherford: A Short Biography: The Father of Nuclear Physics

Index